Rebus Story

Use the key at the right to help with the story.

They knew that  is God's Son.

But some of their leaders did not   .

They took  and nailed him to a  .

 died on the  .

But three days later, on the first  morning,

 rose from the dead.  is alive!

We call this the Resurrection, and we celebrate it every  . What is your favorite thing about  ?

country

Jesus

people

love

cross

Easter

The Sign of the Cross

People from all over the world are followers of Jesus. Unscramble the letters, and fill in the blanks with the word that tells what we receive on Ash Wednesday to show that we are followers of Jesus. Then color a cross on each person's forehead.

S S E A H

_____ _____ _____ _____ _____

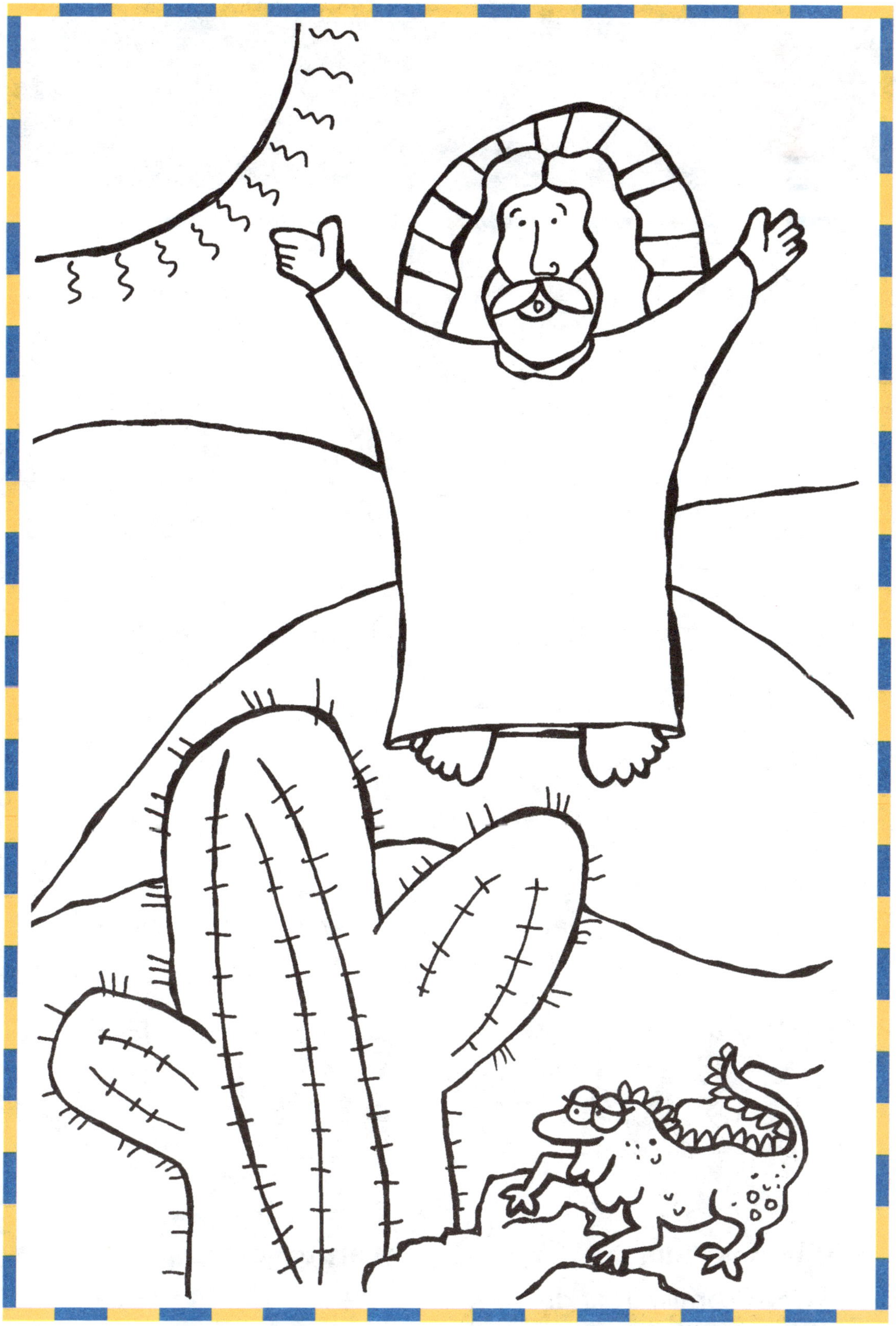

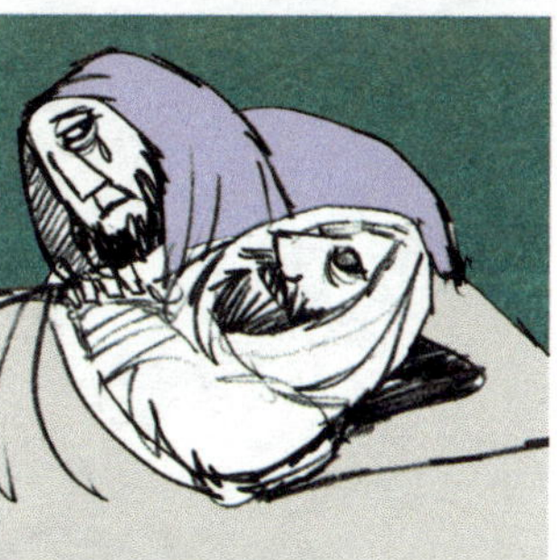

Jesus in the Desert

Color this picture of Jesus. Though he had a tough time in the desert, he still praised God.

3rd Station

14th Station

9th Station

4th Station

11th Station

13th Station

Unscramble

Each year during Lent, we remember the story of how Israel got to the Promised Land. Unscramble the words to find out how, then color the picture.

1. The Israelites were slaves in __ __ __ __ __. gptyE

2. __ __ __ __ __ __ led them out of slavery. ssoeM

3. They wandered in the __ __ __ __ __ __. deesrt

4. They crossed the __ __ __   __ __ __. edR eaS

5. It took them __ __ __ __ __ years to get to the Promised Land. rtfoy

6. Lent has forty __ __ __ __ in memory of the Israelites' long journey. syad

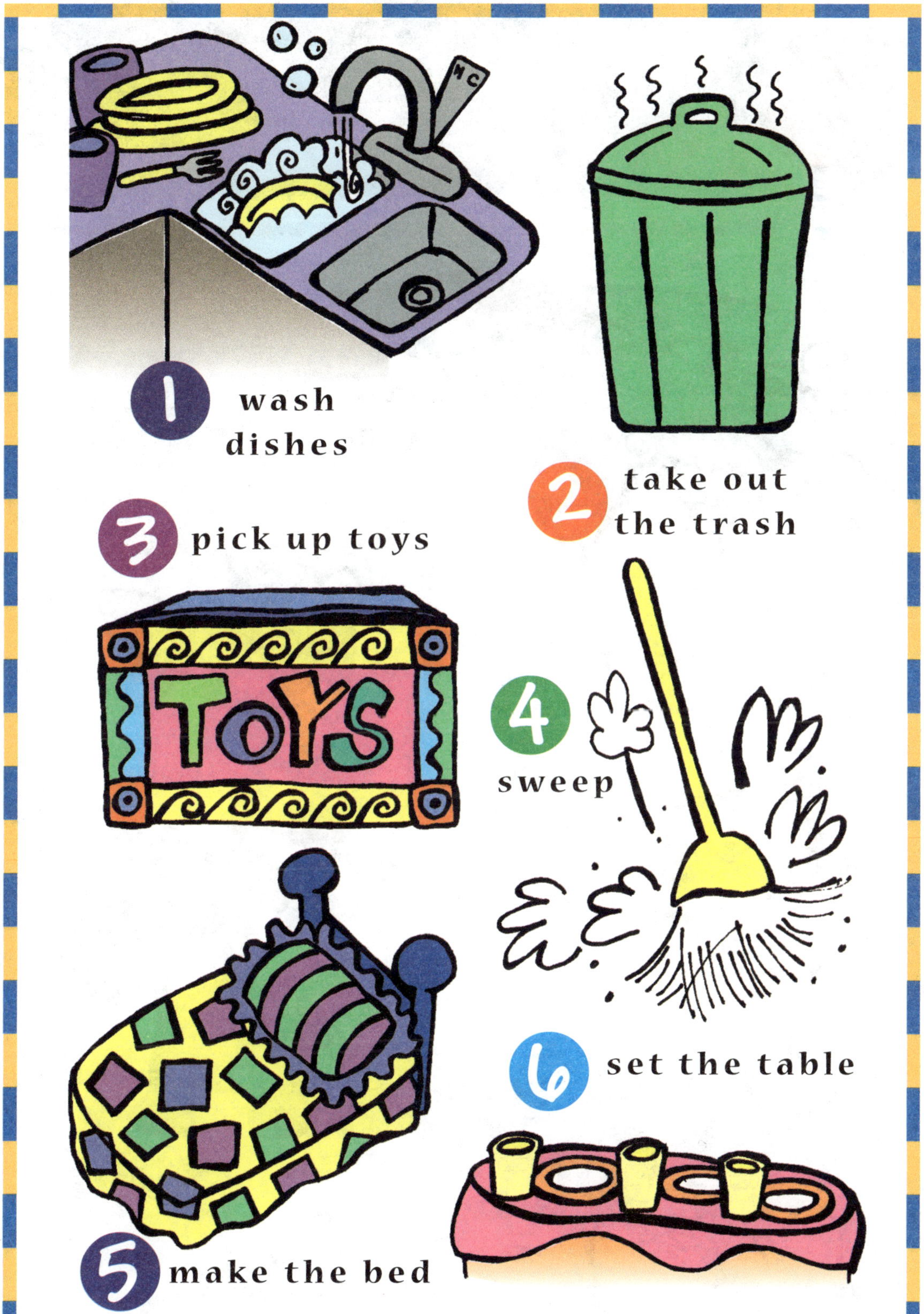

1 wash dishes

2 take out the trash

3 pick up toys

4 sweep

5 make the bed

6 set the table

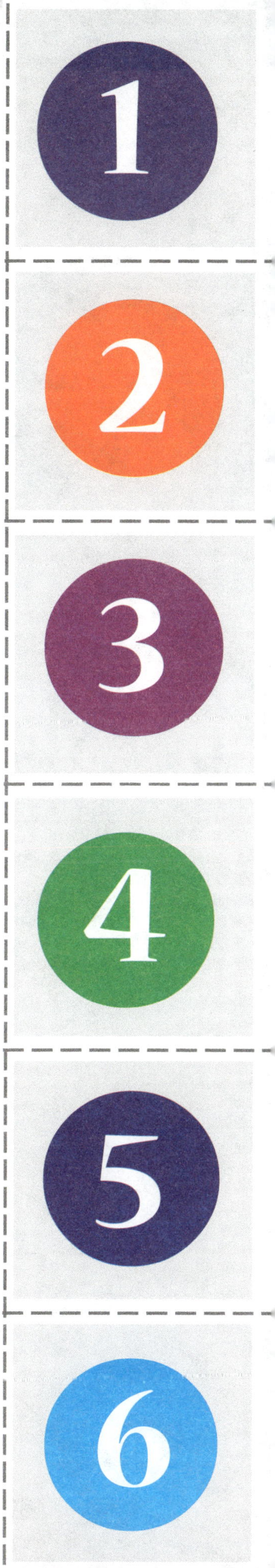

a Game for Lent

Cut out the squares on the right, and shuffle like a deck of cards. Each day, draw a new card and do the action that matches the number. Invite other members of your family to play this lenten game with you.

Word Game

Spell the word that matches the picture. Then write each letter in the numbered blank below to find the message.

_ _ _
1 2 8

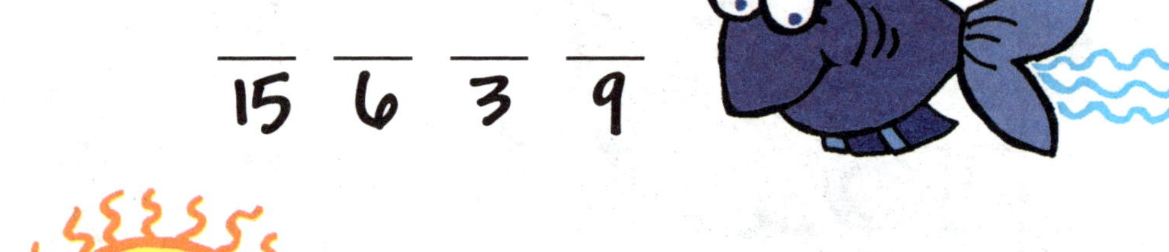

_ _ _ _
15 6 3 9

_ _ _
11 4 13

_ _ _
18 14 16

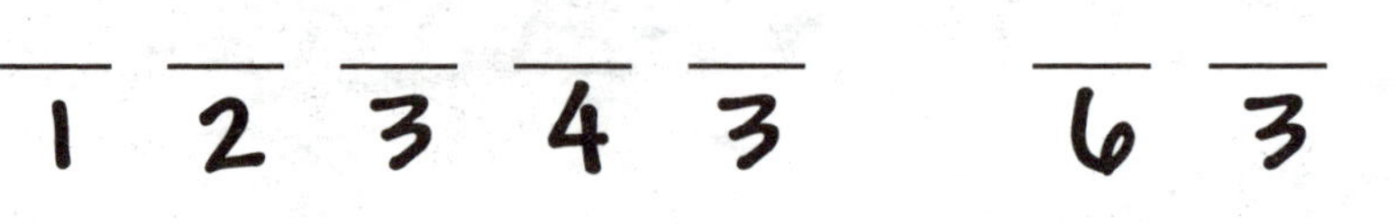

_ _ _ _ _   _ _
1 2 3 4 3   6 3

_ _ _   _ _ _
8 9 2   11 14 13

_ _   _ _ _
14 15   16 14 18

SARAH, LOOK AT ME!

JACOB, COME DOWN AND SEE WHAT ABRAHAM FOUND!

Baby Chick Search

Find all the baby chicks. HINT: You should find 8.

Kindness Stamp

Calendar: Holy Thursday

Calendar: Passion Sunday

Calendar: Good Friday

Calendar: Easter Sunday

Calendar: Easter Vigil

DIRECTIONS

Noah's Ark Color by Number

1=Gray; 2= Dark Blue; 3=Light Blue; 4=Dark Green; 5=Yellow; 6=Brown; 7=Pink; 8=Red; 9=Orange; 10=Black; 11=Purple

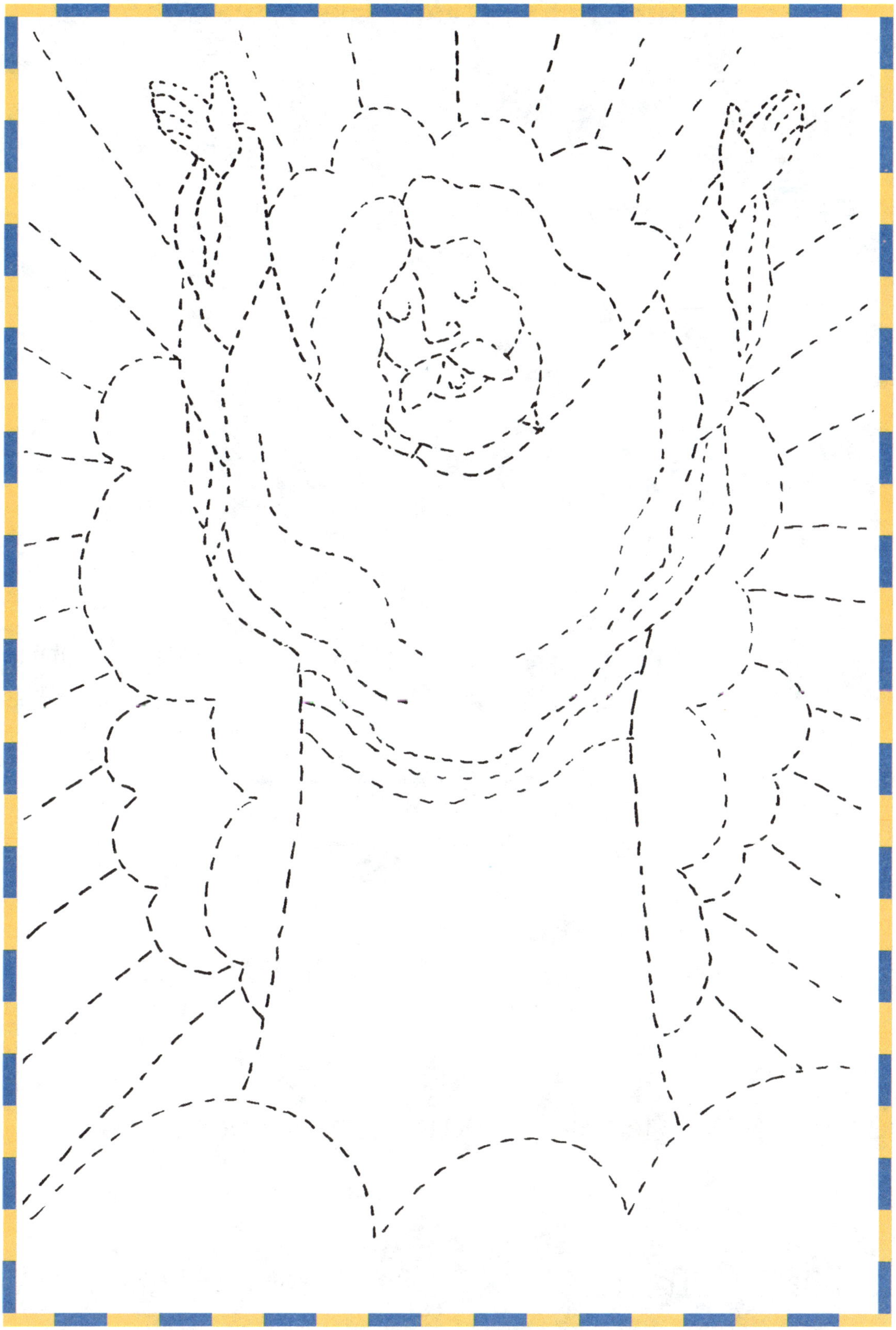

The Transfiguration

Trace the dotted lines, and color the picture.

The Transfiguration

 took his , Peter, James, and John,

up to the top of a high .

All of a sudden,  changed. His face was as

bright as the , and his clothes shone with

a white light. Then  came and talked

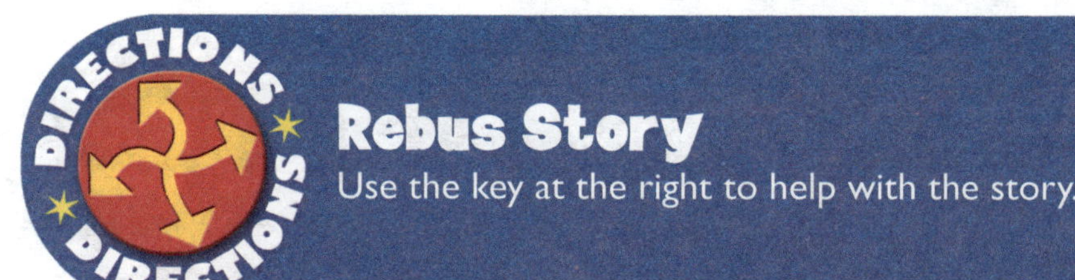

Rebus Story

Use the key at the right to help with the story.

with  . A bright  came over them.

From the  came a great voice: "This is

my Son, , and I love him. Listen to what he says!"

The  looked around, but they saw

only . As  and the  were

coming down the , told them

to say nothing about what they had seen.

Jesus

disciples

mountain

sun

Moses and Elijah

cloud

Crossword Puzzle

Write the name of the numbered pictures in the correct squares to complete the puzzle.

5. down

4. down

3. across

4. across

2. down

1. across

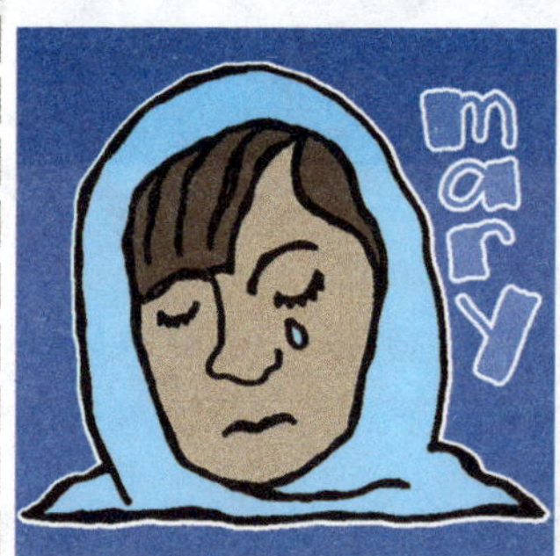

N T P Q H I B E I R
S V H O I E X Z S
A M U F K C L Z Y E
K C N I R H C X J O V
S W N E O J L E N O
V S C E O Q H N . I M
L N I G F S A M T N
E E J N L X T W O Y
P W A M H Y A S G T
B Q H R C E Y V E S
A X Z M U Y S . D U

____ ____ ____ ____   ____ ____   ____ ____

____ ____ ____ ____ ____ ____   ____ ____ ____.

____ ____ ____ ____ ____ ____   ____ ____

____ ____ ____ ____   ____ ____

____ ____ ____ ____.

Secret Message

Circle the blue letters to find God's message to you. Write it on the blank lines.

Secret Message

Write the letters on the lines below, but skip the Zs. What message do you see?

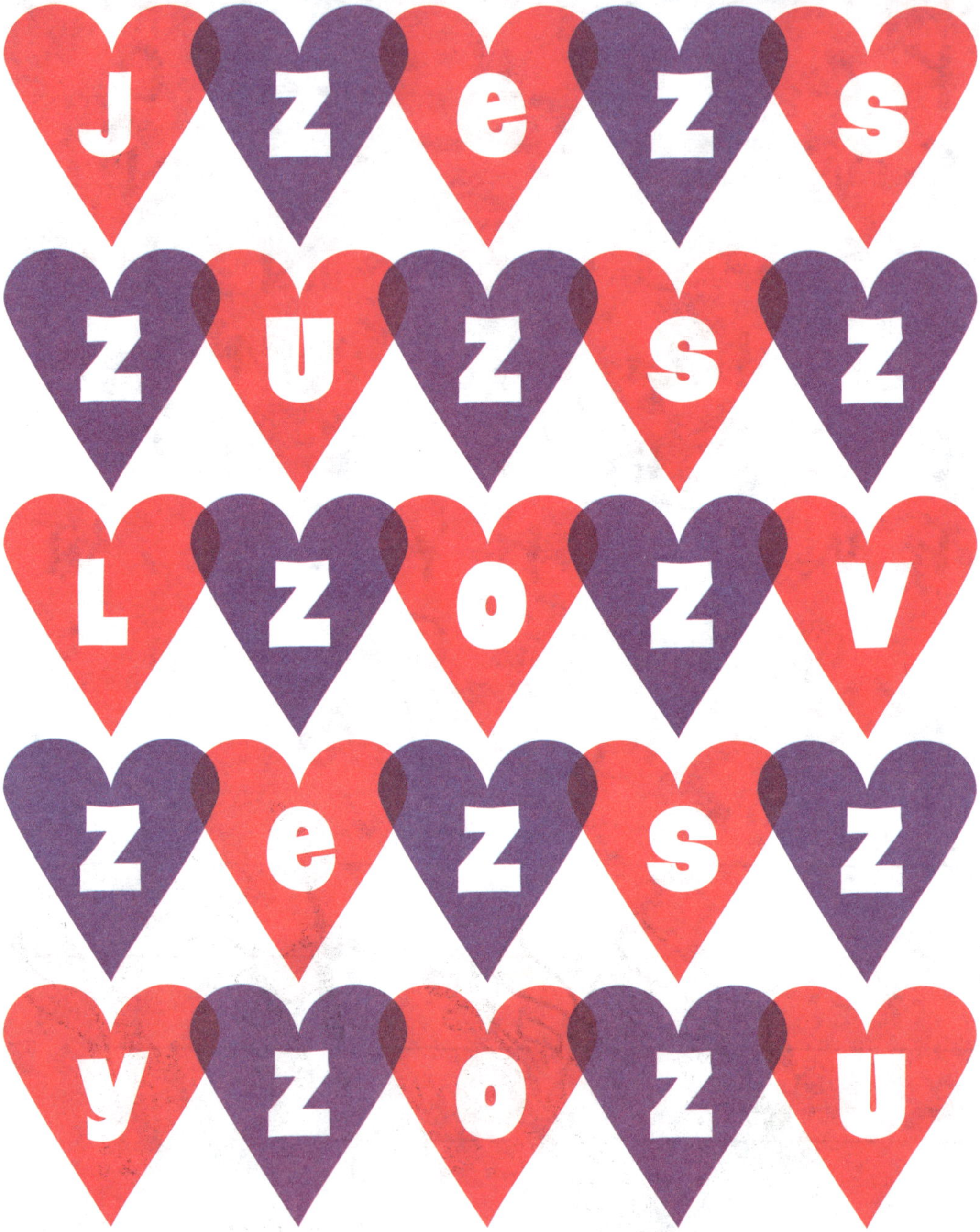

J Z e Z s
Z U Z s Z
L Z o Z v
Z e Z s Z
y Z o Z U

___ ___ ___ ___ ___

___ ___ ___ ___ ___   ___ ___ ___

6th Station

10th Station

5th Station

God Comes to Us

God came to Moses in a burning bush. Sometimes God comes to us through kind people, a beautiful sunset, or joy in our hearts. How does God come to you? Draw a picture of your meeting with God.

Jesus Tells a Story

Jesus liked to tell stories so his friends could understand God's great love for us. Cut out the pieces at the left, and paste in the center to make a picture of the story Jesus told about the fig tree.

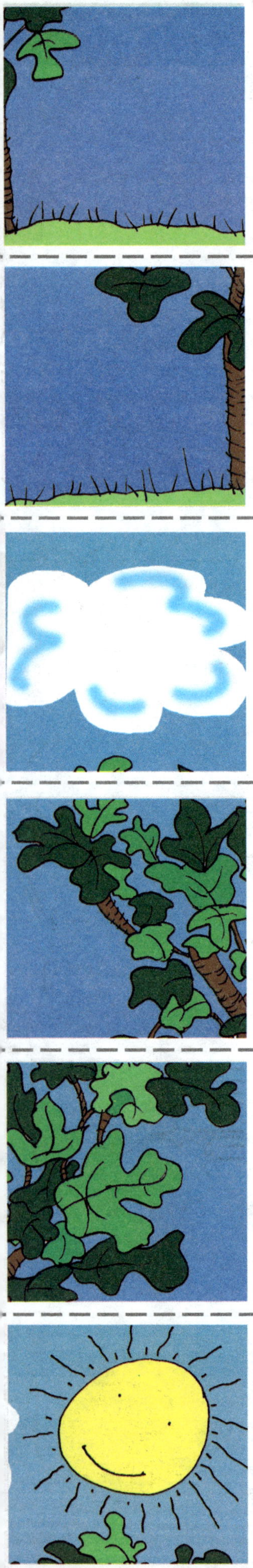

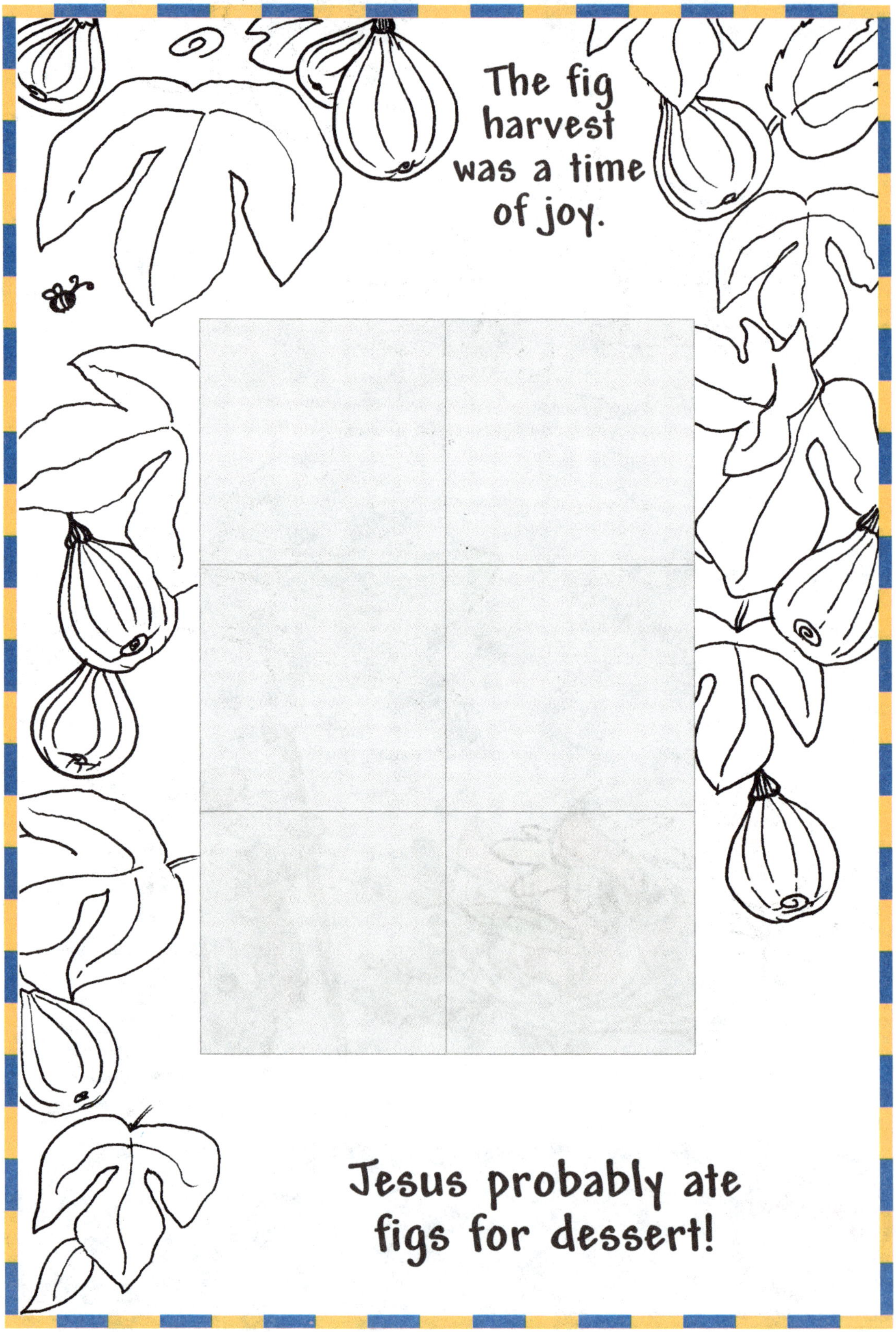

The fig harvest was a time of joy.

Jesus probably ate figs for dessert!

TUBTRELYF

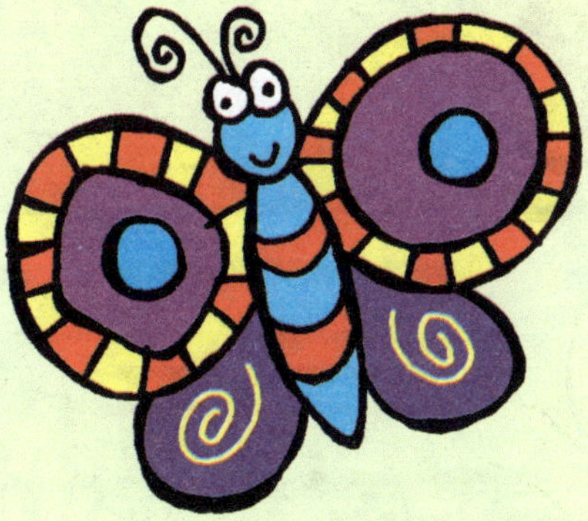

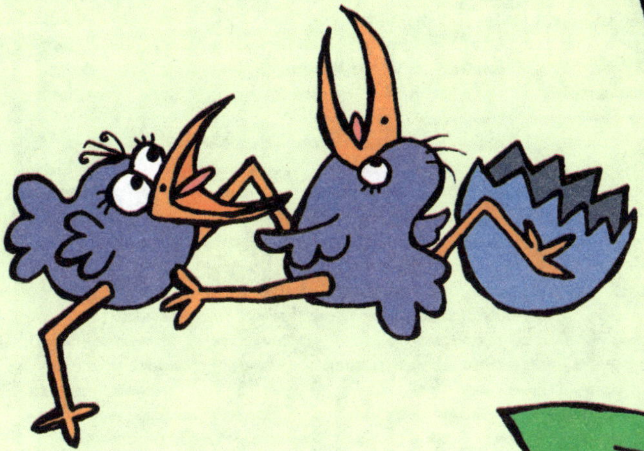

____

BBAY IRBDS

____

____

REGEN VEALES

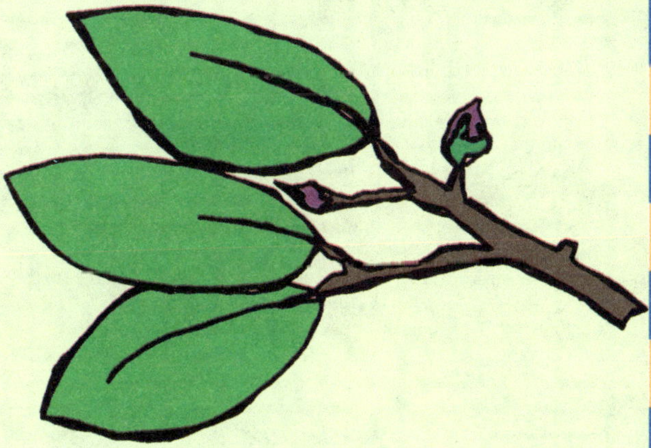

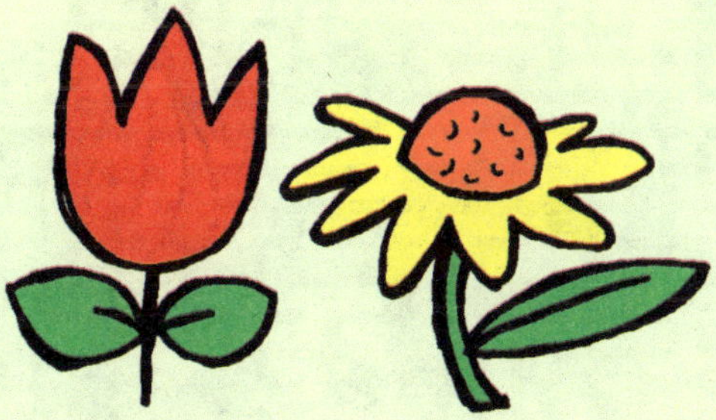

____

____

LFWORES

____

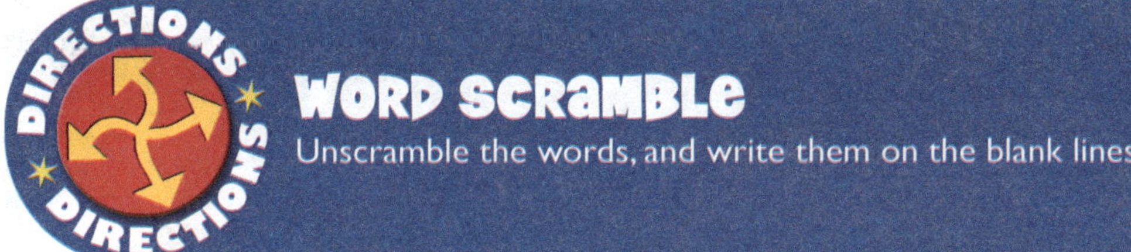

WORD SCRAMBLE

Unscramble the words, and write them on the blank lines.

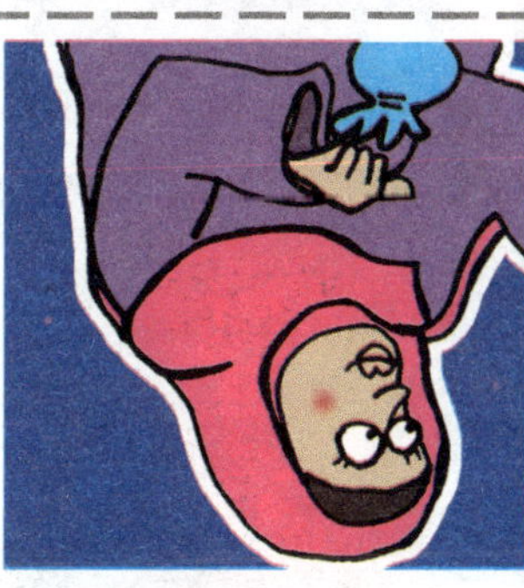

Picture Scramble Page 23

Picture Scramble Page 23

Picture Scramble Page 23

Picture Scramble Page 23

Picture Scramble Page 23

Picture Scramble Page 23

Journey Through the Maze

Help the Jewish people find their way from slavery in Egypt to freedom in the Promised Land.

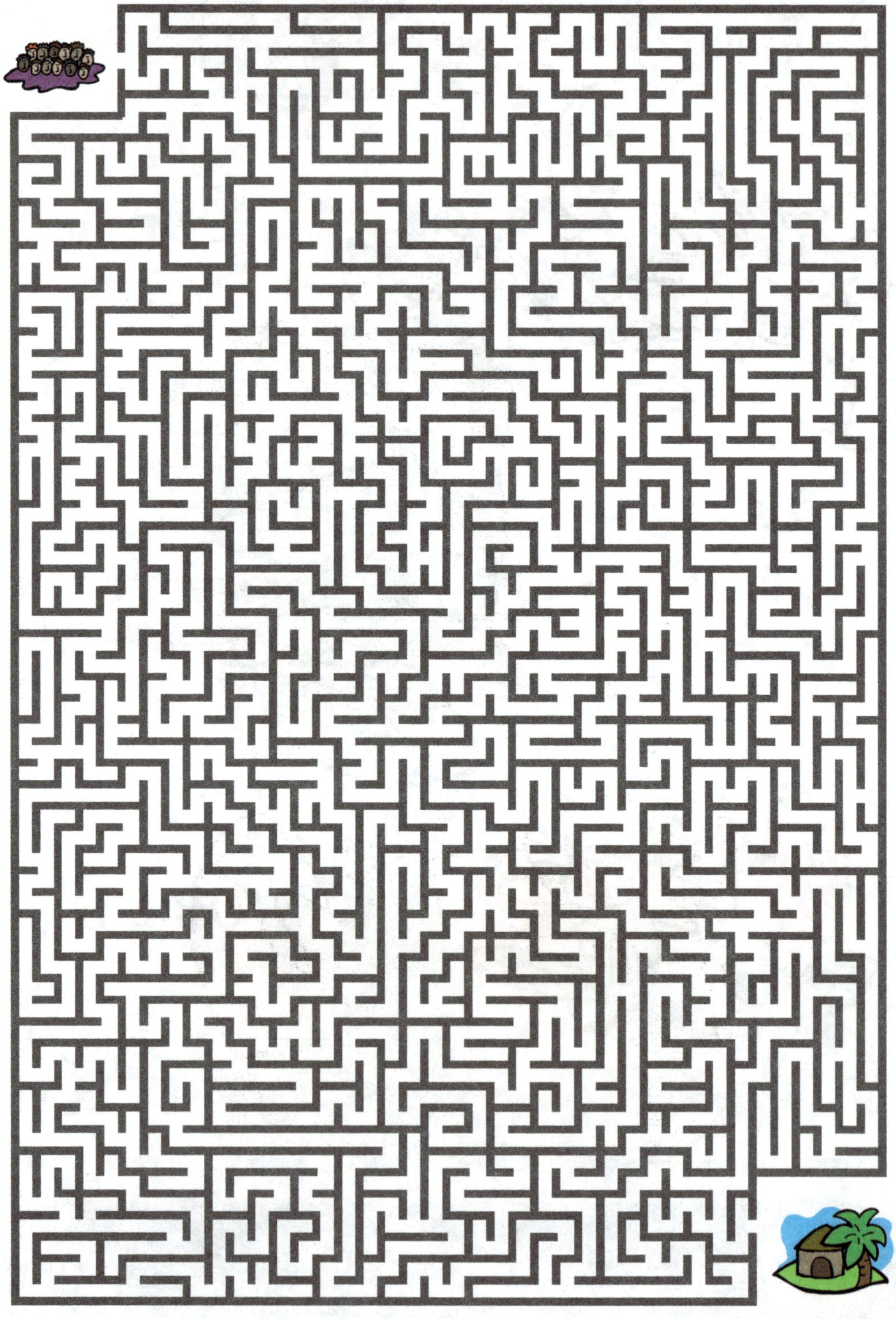

How to play...

After cutting out all the cards, shuffle them, and pass each player a card until all the cards are gone. (Don't let anyone see your cards.) First lay all your matching pairs down. Then, each person takes a turn drawing a card from the player to the left. Keep drawing cards until everyone matches all of their cards except one.

The person with that card left at the end must tell everyone what picture is on the card.

Lenten Card Game

Cut out all 33 cards needed for this game. The cards can be found on pages 11, 15, 29, 31, 35, and 39. The cards have a picture on one side and a blue pattern on the back.

Ten Commandments

Ten Commandments

Ten Commandments

Ten Commandments

Ten Commandments

Ten Commandments

Do not misuse my name.

Respect your father and your mother.

Do not steal.

Do not tell lies about others.

Do not want what belongs to others.

Do not worship other gods.

DIRECTIONS

Ten Commandments

Cut out the commandments, and paste them below the correct numeral. Which one is most important to you today? Draw a circle around that one.

The Prodigal Son

The Widow's Coin

The Good Samaritan

Picture Scramble

Tear out the stamps on page 19, and match the pairs that come from Jesus' stories of the Prodigal Son, the Widow's Coin, and the Good Samaritan. Glue them in the right places.

Lenten Calendar

Sunday and Holy Week stamps are found on other pages. Find them, cut them out, and paste them in the correct boxes. On the days that have no picture, draw a picture of something you thank God for on that day.

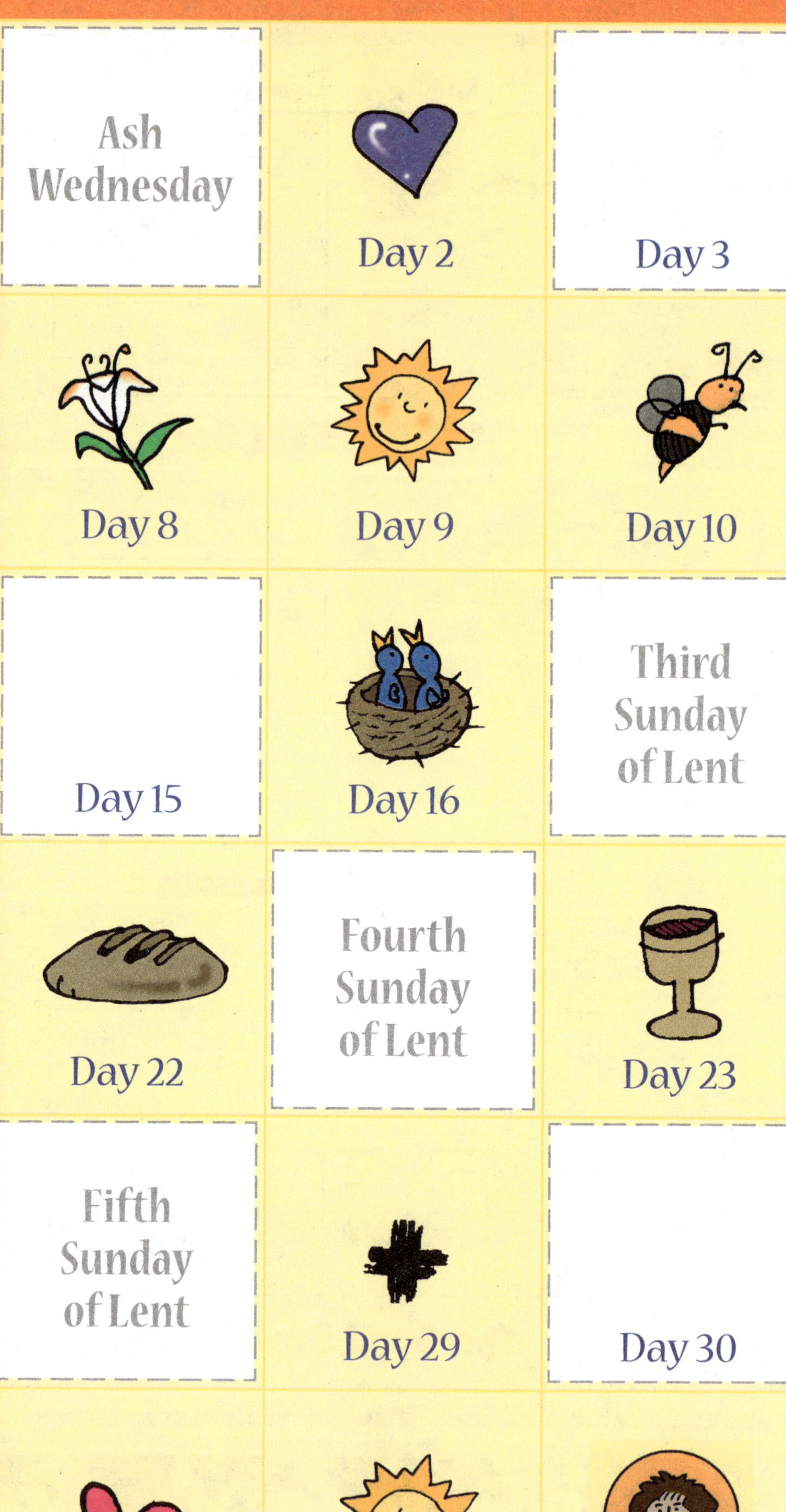

ay 4
First Sunday of Lent
Day 5
Day 6
Day 7
ay 11
Second Sunday of Lent
Day 12
Day 13
Day 14
ay 17
Day 18
Day 19
Day 20
Day 21
ay 24
Day 25
Day 26
Day 27
Day 28
ay 31
Day 32
Day 33
Day 34
Passion Sunday
oly ursday
Good Friday
Easter Vigil
Easter Sunday

Rebus Story

Use the keys to help with the story.

book

dishes

park

Hint: Read the time.

glue

It was  's  to do . 

had a  game at the . The game was

at , and it was already .

 asked , "Will you do the 

for  to ?"  answered, "I want to

read my  to . Why doesn't  do

her own ?"  said to ,

"  has a  game at the .

Will you do her  for her this time?"

 refused. "All right, ," said .

"You go to the  game with your  and I

will do the ." So and went to

the game, did the ,

and read his . Later saw that

the cover was torn. He came out to the kitchen.

was still doing the . " ," he asked,

"Will you my cover for me?" looked

at and then said, " , when I asked you for a

favor for , you wouldn't do it. Why should I your

for you?" thought about that for a while.

Then he said, " , I'm sorry I didn't help . If you

the , I will finish the ."

What important lesson did learn?

Saint Paul's Journey

Saint Paul traveled far to tell as many people as he could about God's peace and forgiveness. Connect the dots to follow Saint Paul on his second journey from Asia Minor to Europe and back again.

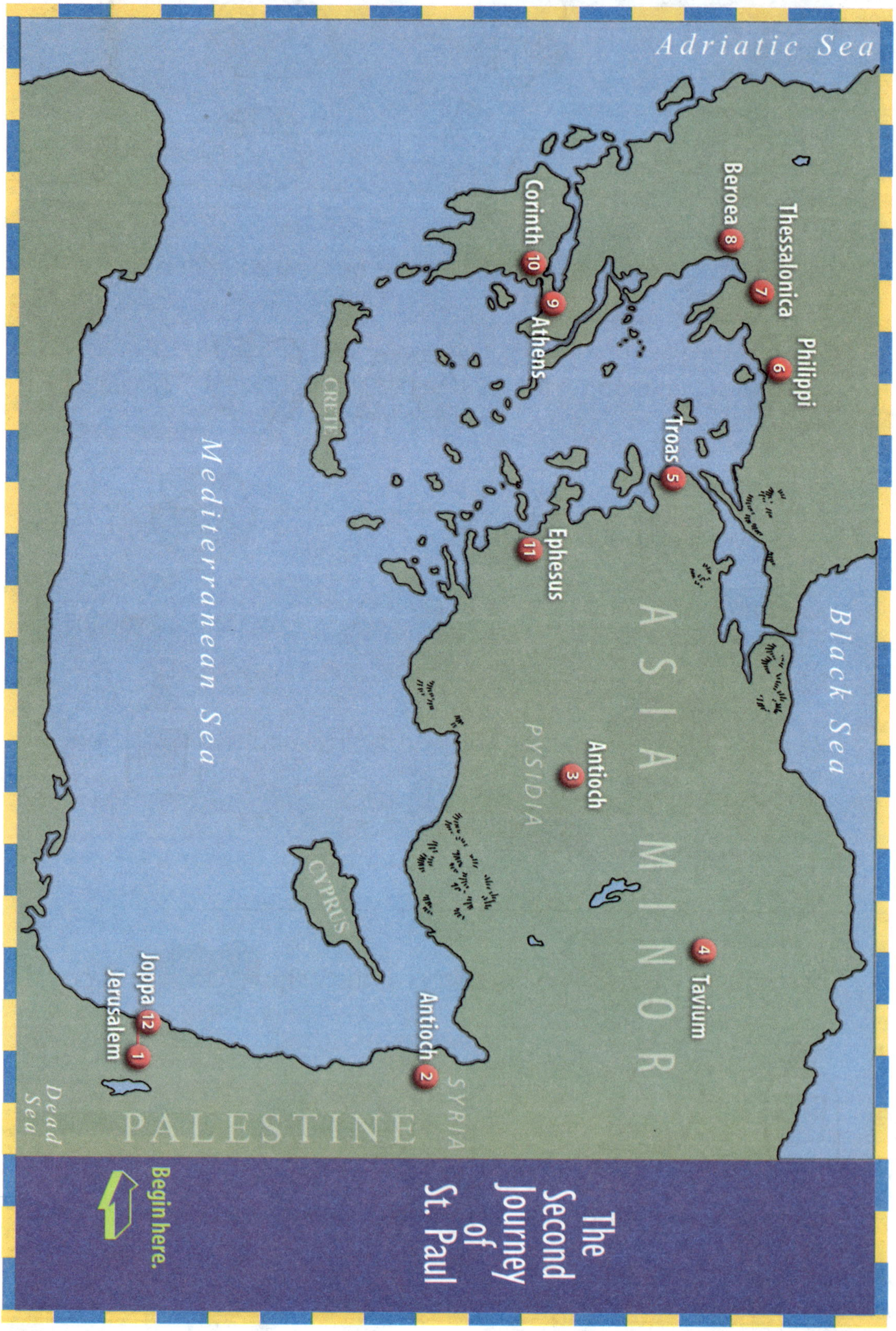

The Second Journey of St. Paul

Begin here.

1 Jerusalem
2 Antioch
3 Antioch
4 Tavium
5 Troas
6 Philippi
7 Thessalonica
8 Beroea
9 Athens
10 Corinth
11 Ephesus
12 Joppa

Adriatic Sea
Mediterranean Sea
Black Sea
Dead Sea
ASIA MINOR
PYSIDIA
PALESTINE
SYRIA
CRETE
CYPRUS

(Name)

Is Like Jesus Because

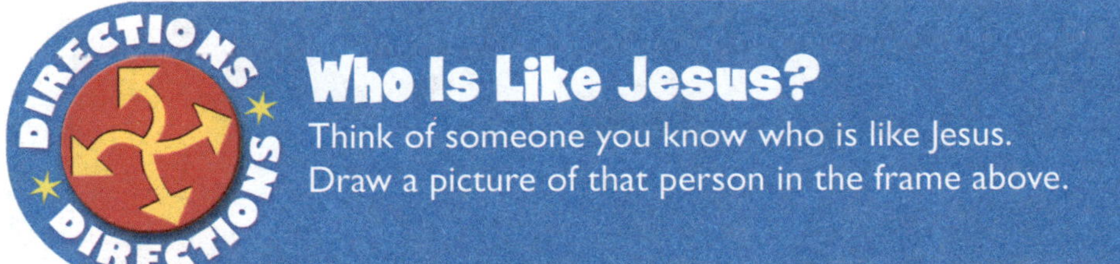

Who Is Like Jesus?

Think of someone you know who is like Jesus.
Draw a picture of that person in the frame above.

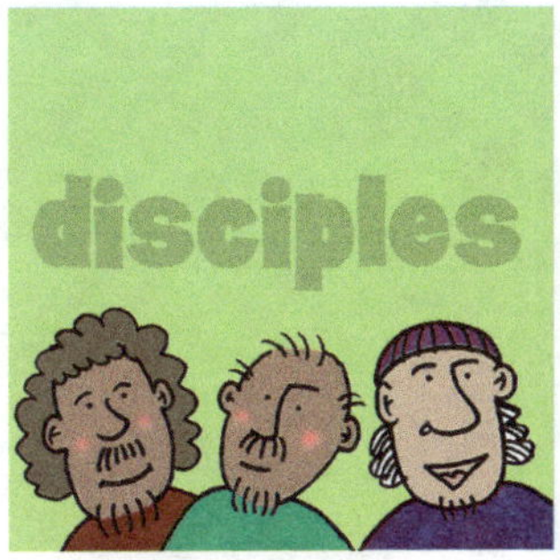

Sign of the Cross

We show that we love God by making the Sign of the Cross. Color the cross, and then make the Sign of the Cross on yourself as you say the prayer.

[Touch forehead]

In the name of the Father,

[Touch chest]

and of the Son,

[Touch left shoulder]

and of the Holy

[Touch right shoulder]

Spirit.

Jesus Loves Children

a picture to color

Jesus loves us, and he forgives us when we have done something wrong. As you color this picture, remember a time when forgiveness has lightened your heart.

God Gives Us Hope

When we feel discouraged, God has a message for us. To decode the message, match the letter in the top row of the key to the letter underneath it. Fill in each blank with the new letter. Now you can see how God gives us hope.

D	E	F	G	H	I	J	K	L	M	N	O	P	Q	R	S	T	U	V	W	X	Y	Z	A	B	C
A	B	C	D	E	F	G	H	I	J	K	L	M	N	O	P	Q	R	S	T	U	V	W	X	Y	Z

____ ' ___ ____ ____ ____ _____

GRQW WKLQN DERXW

___ _____. _ __

WKH SDVW. L DP

____

FUHDWLQJ

_________ ___

VRPHWKLQJ QHZ.

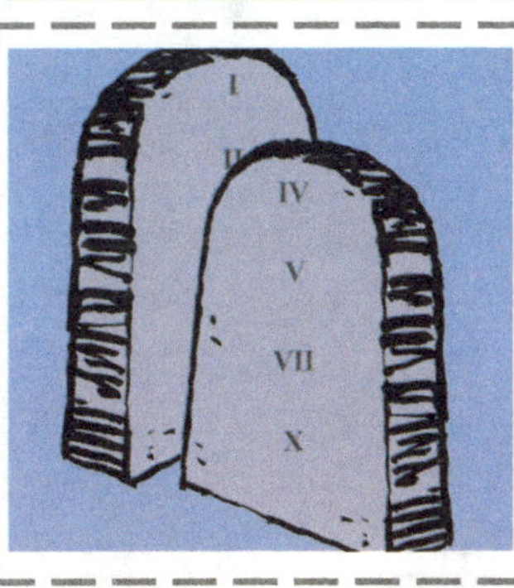

Secret Message

Find the hidden word by coloring in all the boxes that have a purple dot in them. Who is our Savior?

Calendar: Ash Wednesday

Calendar: Second Sunday of Lent

Calendar: First Sunday of Lent

Calendar: Fourth Sunday of Lent

Calendar: Third Sunday of Lent

Calendar: Fifth Sunday of Lent

DIRECTIONS

a-Maze-ing Cross

Follow the maze to reach the center of the cross.

A	X	L	Q	D	Z
S	W	E	S	O	S
U	T	N	P	N	S
S	L	T	Y	K	O
E	A	S	T	E	R
J	E	G	G	Y	C

EGG

JESUS

LENT

EASTER

CROSS

DONKEY

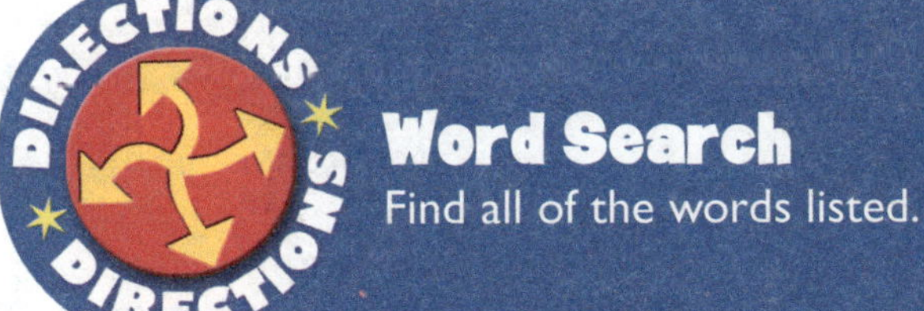

Word Search
Find all of the words listed.

Hidden Palms

These children want to welcome Jesus into Jerusalem by waving their palm branches. How many branches can you count?

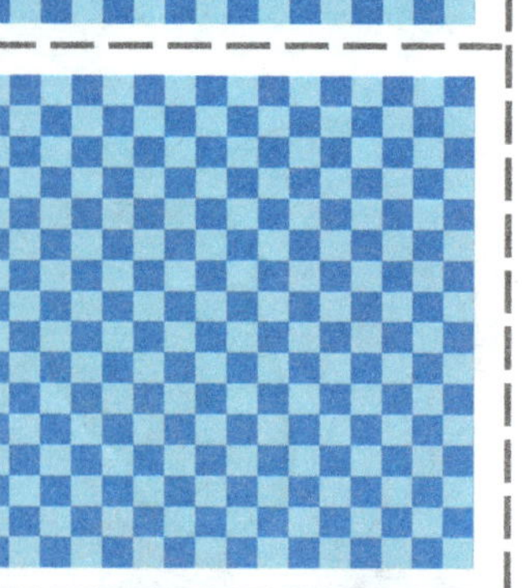

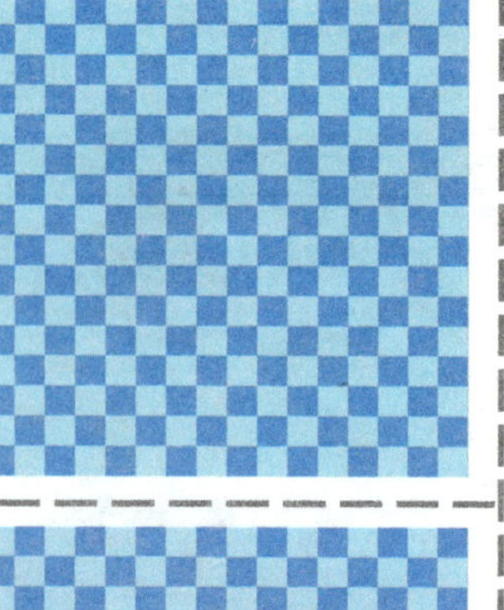

Jesus died on the...

Jesus rode to Jerusalum on a...

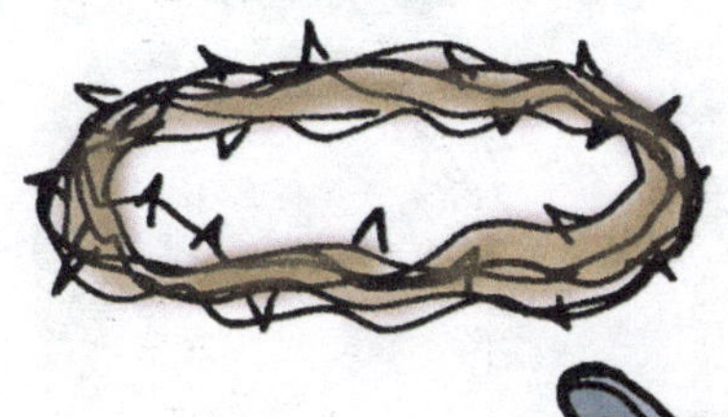

In Jerusalem people cheered and waved...

Jesus wore a...

These things were driven in Jesus' feet and hands...

Picture Scramble

Picture Scramble

Picture Scramble

Picture Scramble

Picture Scramble

Picture Scramble

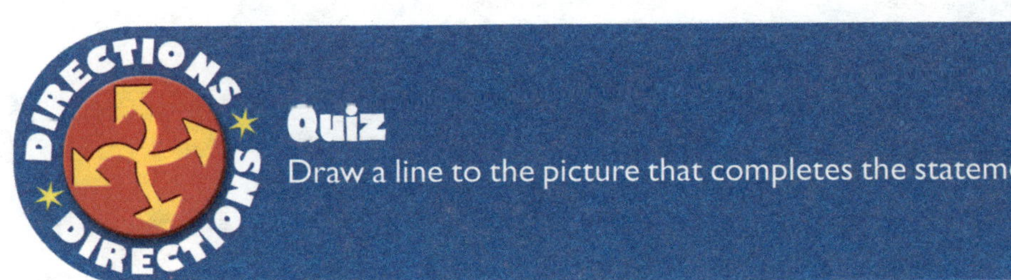

Quiz

Draw a line to the picture that completes the statement correctly.

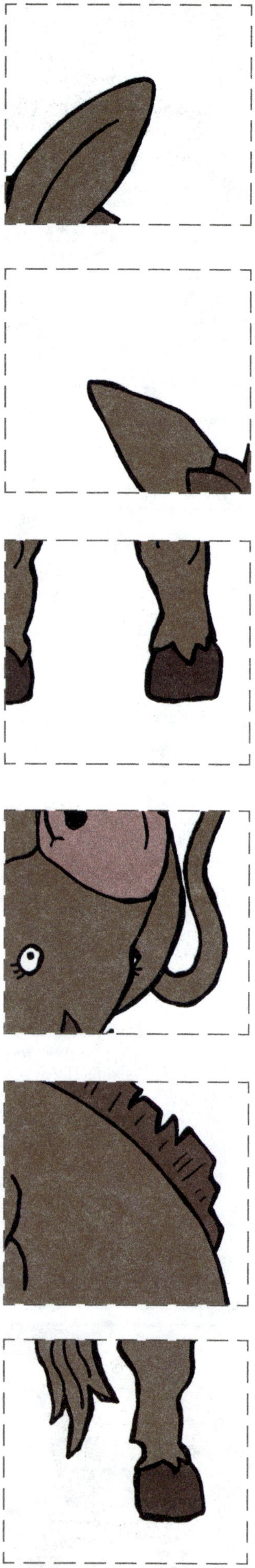

Picture Scramble

Who carried Jesus into Jerusalem? Put the pieces together to find out.

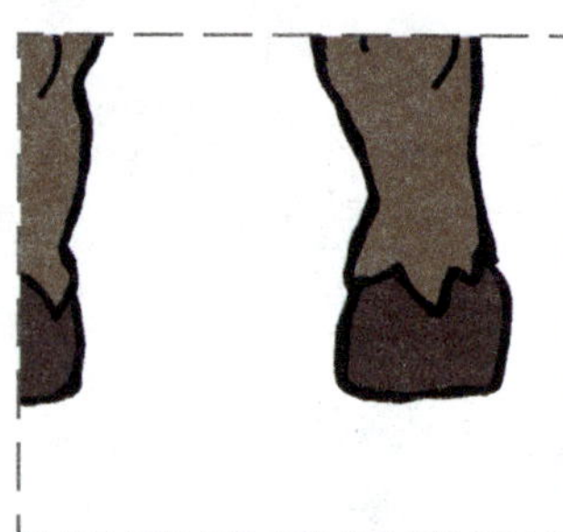

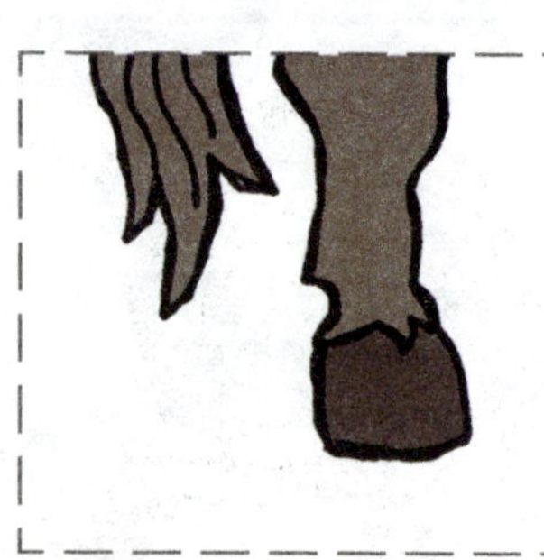

"This is my body that is for you."

The Last Supper

Color the picture of Jesus sharing Eucharist with his friends.

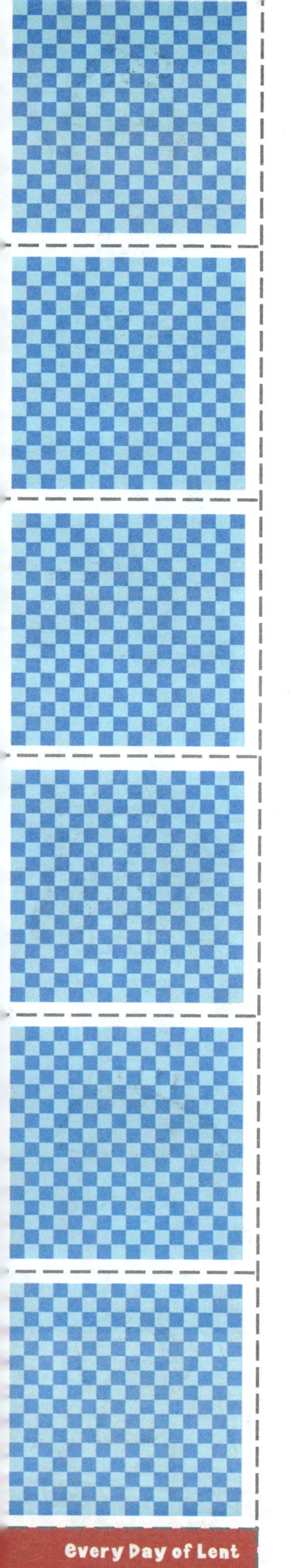

 's father Jacob owned a .

One day Jacob said to , "Tonight 

and his  will have their supper in

the ." All that day  and his

father worked hard cleaning the .

Then they went to the market and bought 

and  for  and his .

That evening,  and his  came to the  for their supper.  and his father served the  and  and other food. When supper was over,  took some  and gave it to his  saying, "This is my body."  also took some  and gave it to his  saying, "This is my blood." As  stood waiting to serve, he thought, "What a wonderful gift  is giving to his ! He is not just giving them  and ,  is giving himself to his ." Then  turned around and saw  waiting quietly.  said to , "Would you like to be my disciple too?"

What do you think  said?

Rebus Key

Joshua

banquet room

disciples

Jesus

bread

wine

The Way of the Cross

Follow Jesus on his Way of the Cross by cutting out the stations and pasting them in order.

Then beginning with the first station, go to each one saying this prayer:

We adore you, O Christ,
and we praise you,
because by your holy cross
you have redeemed the world.

Finish each station by praying your own prayer of love to Jesus from your heart.

1

Jesus is condemned to die.

2

Jesus takes up his cross.

3

Jesus falls the first time.

4

Jesus meets his mother.

5

Simon helps Jesus carry his cross.

6

Veronica wipes the face of Jesus.

7

Jesus falls the second time.

8

Jesus meets the crying women.

9

Jesus falls the third time.

10

Jesus is stripped of his garments.

11

Jesus is nailed to the cross.

12

Jesus dies on the cross.

13

Jesus is taken down from the cross.

14

Jesus is buried in the tomb.

Jesus is risen.

8th Station

12th Station

2nd Station

7th Station

Jesus is risen.

1st Station

DIRECTIONS

Jesus Shows Us How to Love

Jesus carried his cross out of love for us, although it was very difficult for him. What difficult thing have you done out of love for someone else? Write about it on the lines below.

paschal candle

chrism

baptismal water

fire

baptismal garment

bells

Help Celebrate the Easter Vigil

DIRECTIONS

Help your parish get ready to celebrate Jesus' Resurrection by learning the names of the symbols we use at the Easter Vigil Mass. Find the right words to describe each symbol, cut out the words, and paste them near the right picture.

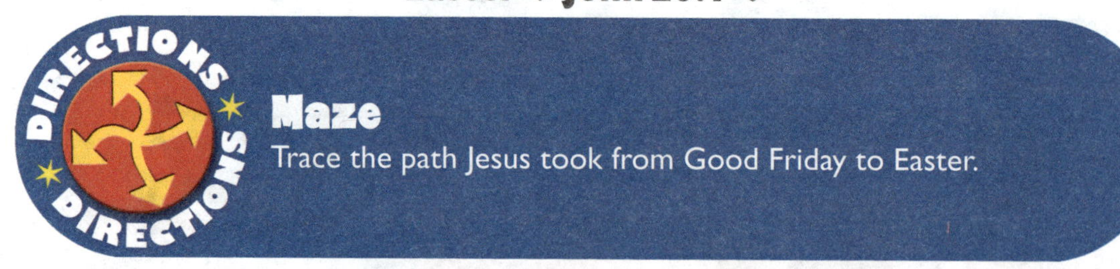

Maze

Trace the path Jesus took from Good Friday to Easter.

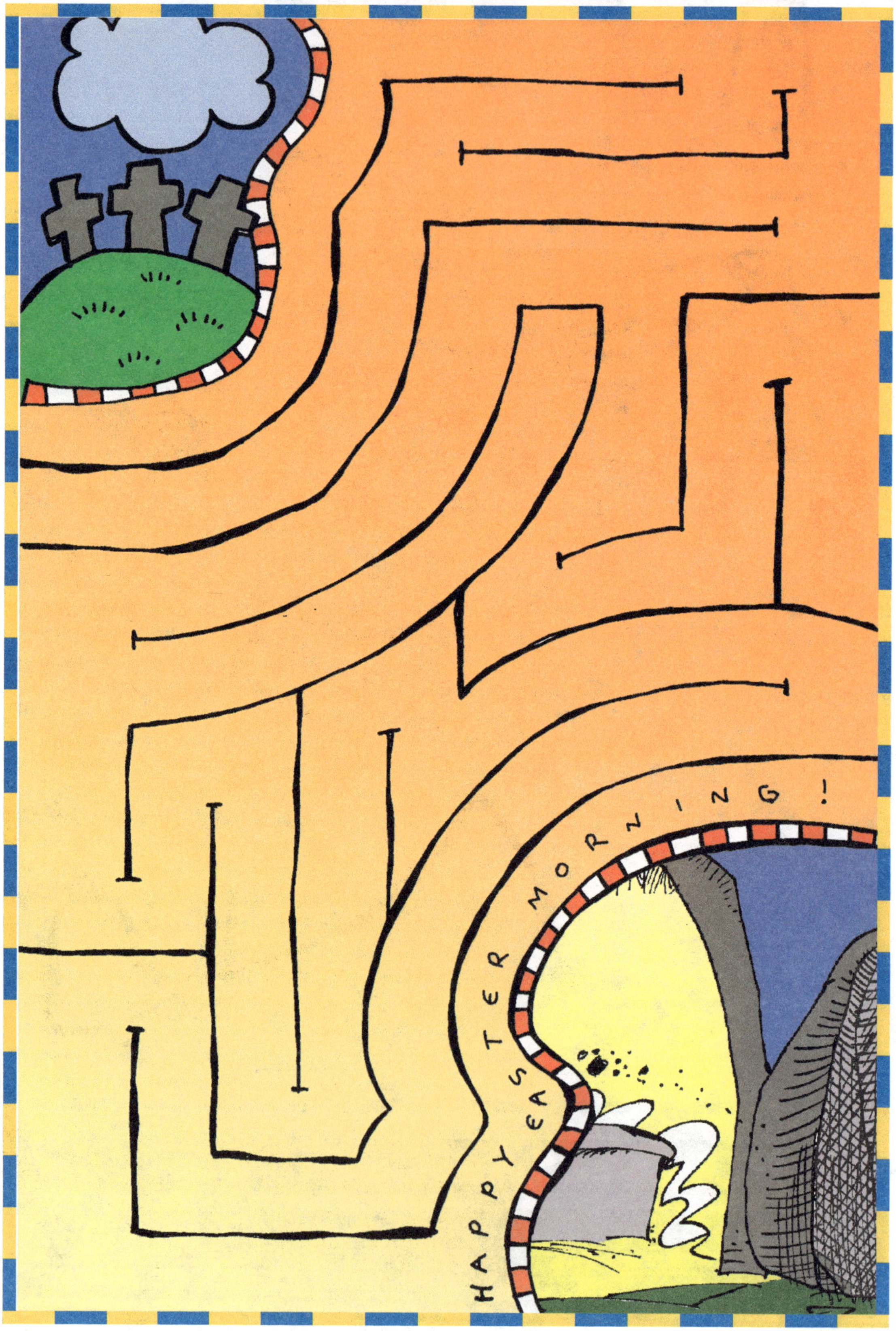

HAPPY EASTER MORNING!